# Comparing Segments

1. **Check:** Which segment is longest? _ _ _ _ _ _

   Which segment is shortest? _ _ _ _ _ _ _

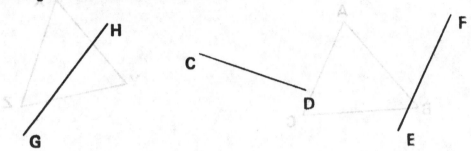

2. **Check:** Are the segments congruent? _ _ _ _ _ _

3. **Construct a segment $\overline{UV}$ congruent to $\overline{AB}$ on the given line.**

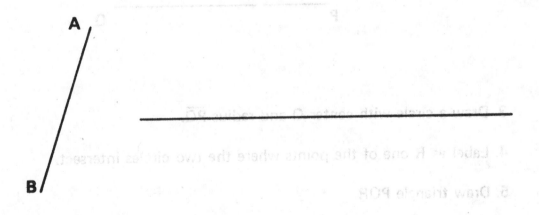

1. Which triangle is equilateral? _ _ _ _ _

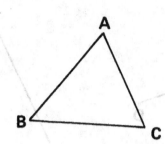
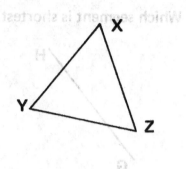

2. Draw a circle with center P and radius $\overline{PQ}$.

P ——————————————— Q

3. Draw a circle with center Q and radius $\overline{PQ}$.

4. Label as R one of the points where the two circles intersect.

5. Draw triangle PQR.

6. Is triangle PQR an equilateral triangle?_ _ _ _ _

   Why? _ _ _ _ _ _ _ _ _ _ _ _ _ _ _ _ _ _ _ _ _ _ _ _

# Key to

# Geometry®

## PERPENDICULARS

**4**
Student
Workbook

By Newton Hawley and Patrick Suppes
Revised by George Gearhart and Peter Rasmussen

Name _____    Class _____

# Key to
# Geometry®
### PERPENDICULARS

**4**
Student Workbook

## TABLE OF CONTENTS

## To the Student

These books will help you to discover for yourself many important relationships of geometry. Your tools will be the same as those used by the Greek mathematicians more than 2000 years ago. These tools are a *compass* and a *straightedge*. In addition, you will need a *sharpened pencil*. The lessons that follow will help you make drawings from which you may learn the most.

The answer books show *one* way the pages may be completed correctly. It is possible that your work is correct even though it is different. If your answer differs, re-read the instructions to make sure you followed them step by step. If you did, you are probably correct.

## About the Cover

Pythagoras was the leader of a secret society in ancient Greece. The society was devoted to the study of music, astronomy, arithmetic, and geometry. Pythagoras and his followers believed that numbers were magical and that the secrets of the universe could be unlocked by studying the relationships between numbers. An Important theorem in geometry is named after Pythagoras. The "Pythagorean Theorem" states that in a right triangle, the sum of the squares on the two short sides equals the square on the long side.

On the cover of this booklet Pythagoras speaks before a meeting of his secret society. The pentagram, or five pointed star, was the symbol of the Pythagoreans.

Cover art by Howard Coale

Printed in the United States of America

Copyright © 1979, 1972 by Holden Day, Inc. All rights reserved.

* *Key to Fractions, Key to Decimals, Key to Percents, Key to Algebra, Key to Geometry, Key to Measurement,* and *Key to Metric Measurement* are registered trademarks of Key Curriculum Press.

Published by Key Curriculum Press, 1150 65th Street, Emeryville, CA 94608

ISBN 978-0-913684-74-0          10 11 12 13 14   LHN  22 21

# Comparing Angles

Problem: *Compare angles.*

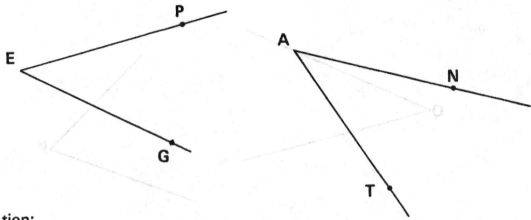

Solution:

1. Draw an arc with center E and radius $\overline{EG}$.

   Make the arc intersect both sides of angle PEG.

2. Draw an arc with center A and radius congruent to $\overline{EG}$ intersecting

   sides $\overrightarrow{AT}$ and $\overrightarrow{AN}$.

   Make the arc intersect both sides of angle NAT.

3. Draw $\overline{PG}$ and $\overline{NT}$.

Rule: *Angle PEG and angle NAT are compared by comparing segments*
   $\overline{PG}$ *and* $\overline{NT}$.

4. Segment $\overline{PG}$ is _ _ _ _ _ _ _ _ _ _ segment $\overline{NT}$.

   (a) longer than          (c) shorter than

   (b) congruent to

5. Angle PEG is _ _ _ _ _ _ _ _ _ _ angle NAT.

   (a) larger than          (c) smaller than

   (b) congruent to

Problem: *Compare angles.*

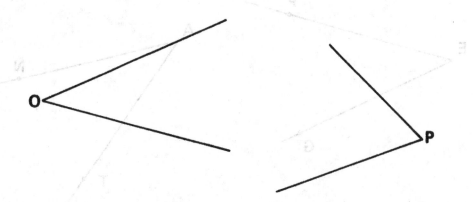

Solution:

1. Draw arcs with congruent radii centered at O and P.

2. Label as A and B the points where the arc with center O intersects the sides of the angle at O.

   Label as X and Y the points where the arc with center P intersects the sides of the angle at P.

Rule: *Compare segments $\overline{AB}$ and $\overline{XY}$ to compare the angles.*

3. The angle at O is _ _ _ _ _ _ _ _ _ _ _ _ the angle at P.

   (a) larger than                    (c) congruent to

   (b) smaller than

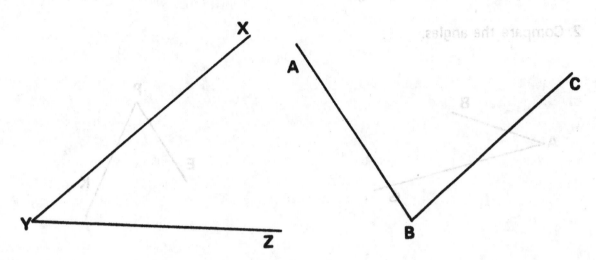

1. Check: Is angle XYZ congruent to angle ABC? _ _ _ _ _

2. Is angle ABC larger than angle XYZ? _ _ _ _ _

3. Is angle XYZ larger than angle ABC? _ _ _ _ _

1. Extend the sides of each angle.

2. Compare the angles.

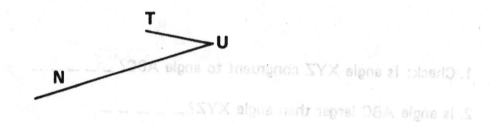

3. The largest angle is _ _ _ _ _.

The second largest angle is _ _ _ _ _.

The smallest angle is _ _ _ _ _.

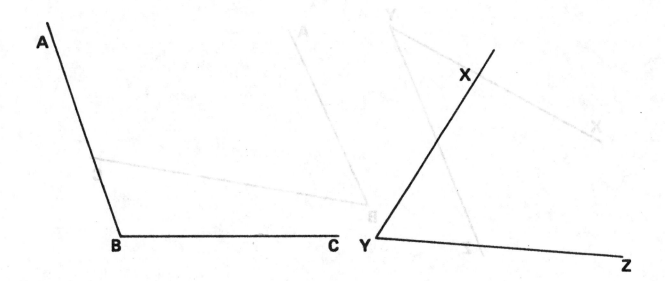

1. Draw an arc with center B to intersect $\overrightarrow{BA}$ and $\overrightarrow{BC}$.

2. Label as D and E the points of intersection of the arc and the rays.

3. Draw $\overline{DE}$.

4. Draw with the same radius an arc with center Y to intersect $\overrightarrow{YX}$ and $\overrightarrow{YZ}$.

5. Label as U and V the points of intersection of the arc and the rays.

6. Draw $\overline{UV}$.

7. Is segment $\overline{DE}$ congruent to segment $\overline{UV}$? _ _ _ _ _

8. Which is longer? _ _ _ _ _

9. Is angle ABC congruent to angle XYZ? _ _ _ _ _

10. Which is larger? _ _ _ _ _

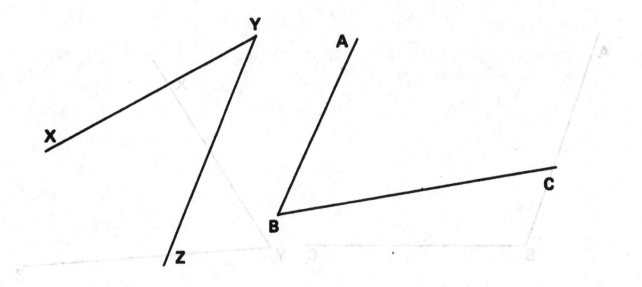

**1. Check:  Is angle ABC congruent to angle XYZ?** _ _ _ _ _

**2. Is angle ABC larger than angle XYZ?** _ _ _ _ _

**3. Is angle ABC smaller than angle XYZ?** _ _ _ _ _

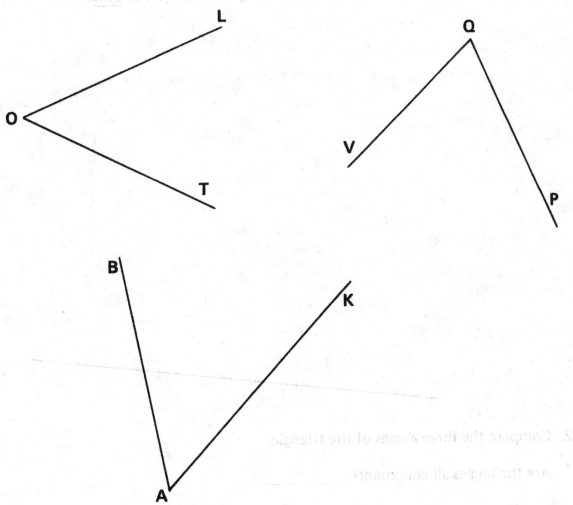

Which angle is the largest? _ _ _ _ _

Which angle is the smallest? _ _ _ _ _

(Use your compass to decide.)

# The Angles of a Triangle

1. Construct an equilateral triangle with the given segment as <u>base</u>.

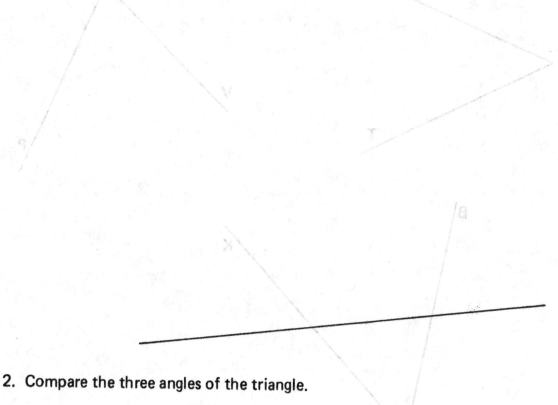

2. Compare the three angles of the triangle.

   Are the angles all congruent? _ _ _ _ _

3. Compare the angles of triangle QRS.

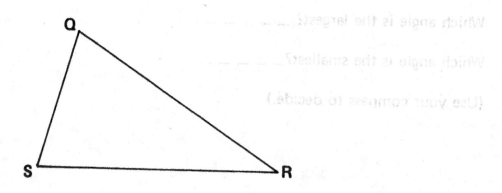

4. Angle RQS is congruent to angle _ _ _ _ _.

5. Side $\overline{RQ}$ is congruent to side _ _ _ _ _.

1. Which is the largest angle in triangle ABC? _ _ _ _ _

2. Which is the largest side? _ _ _ _ _

3. Which is the smallest angle in the triangle? _ _ _ _ _

4. Which is the smallest side? _ _ _ _ _

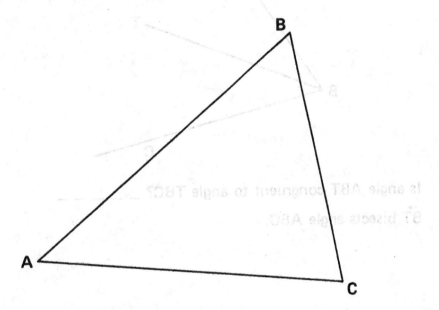

5. Which is the largest angle in triangle DEF? _ _ _ _ _

6. Which is the largest side? _ _ _ _ _

7. Which is the smallest angle in the triangle? _ _ _ _ _

8. Which is the smallest side? _ _ _ _ _

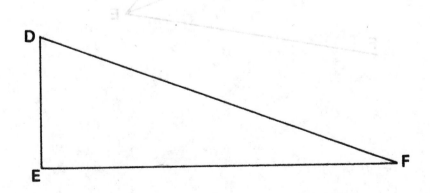

# Bisecting Angles

1. Compare angle ABT and angle TBC.

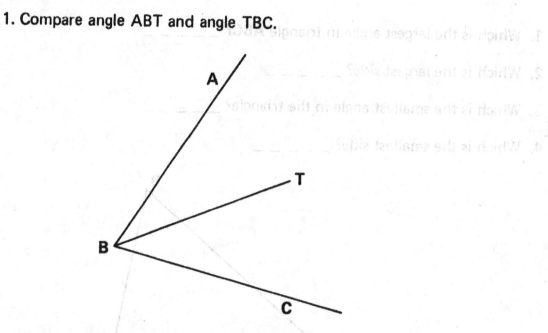

Is angle ABT congruent to angle TBC? _ _ _ _ _

$\overrightarrow{BT}$ bisects angle ABC.

2. Does $\overrightarrow{ER}$ bisect angle DEF? _ _ _ _ _ _

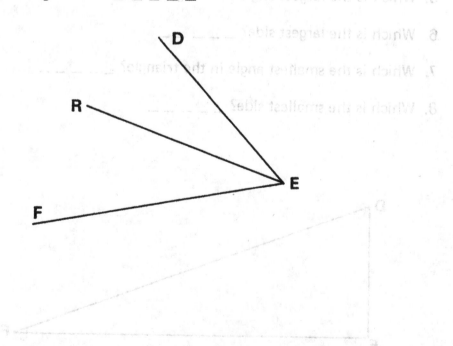

Problem: *Bisect a given angle.*

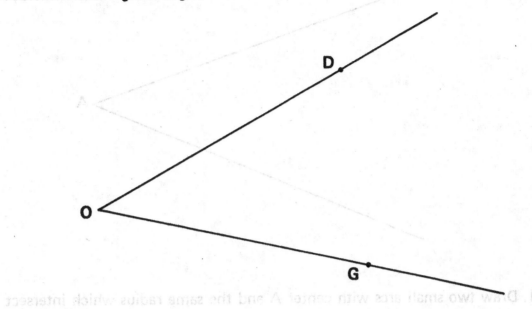

Solution:

1. Draw an arc with center O which passes through D.

2. Draw an arc with center D.

3. Use the same radius to draw an arc with center G.

   Make these arcs intersect.

   Label the point of intersection T.

4. Draw $\overrightarrow{OT}$.

5. Fold your paper on $\overrightarrow{OT}$.

   Is angle DOT congruent to angle GOT? _ _ _ _ _

6. Does $\overrightarrow{OT}$ bisect angle DOG? _ _ _ _ _

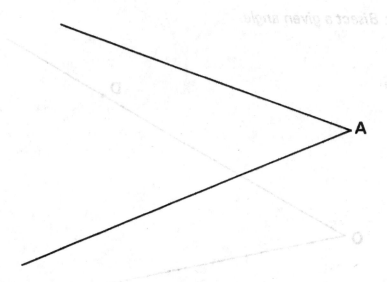

1. Draw two small arcs with center A and the same radius which intersect the sides of the angle.

2. Label the intersections X and Y.

3. Draw an arc with center X.

4. Draw an arc with the same radius and center Y.
   Make these arcs intersect.

5. Label as Z the point of intersection of these arcs.

6. Draw $\overrightarrow{AZ}$.

7. Does $\overrightarrow{AZ}$ bisect angle XAY? _ _ _ _ _ _ _ _

8. Is angle XAZ <u>half</u> of angle XAY? _ _ _ _ _ _ _

# 1. Bisect the angles.

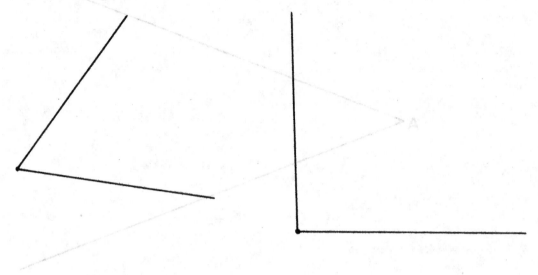

# 2. Bisect the <u>straight angle.</u>

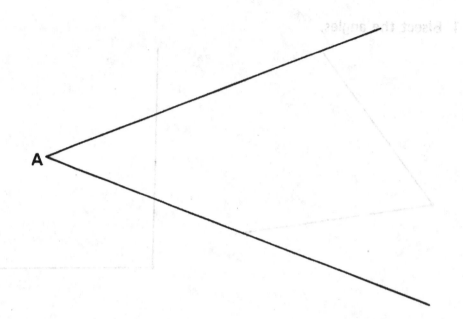

1. Draw small arcs with center A and the same radius which intersect the sides of the angle.

2. Label the intersections X and Y.

3. Draw an arc with center X.

4. Use the same radius to draw an arc with center Y.
   Make the arcs intersect.

5. Label their intersection B.

6. Draw ray $\overrightarrow{AB}$.

7. Now use a longer radius to draw an arc with center X.

8. Use the same radius to draw an arc with center Y.
   Make the arcs intersect.

9. Call their intersection C.

10. Is point C on ray $\overrightarrow{AB}$? _ _ _ _ _

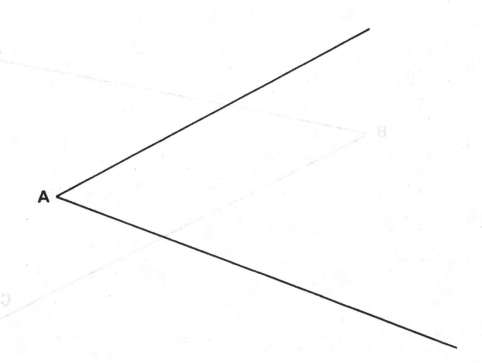

A

1. Draw two small arcs with center A and the same radius which intersect the sides of the angle.

2. Label the points of intersection X and Y.

3. Draw an arc with center X.

4. Draw an arc with the same radius and center Y.

5. Label as Z the point of intersection of these arcs.

6. Draw $\overrightarrow{AZ}$.

7. Then draw $\overline{XZ}$ and $\overline{YZ}$.

8. Fold your paper on $\overrightarrow{AZ}$.

Are segments $\overline{XZ}$ and $\overline{YZ}$ congruent? _ _ _ _ _

Are triangle AXZ and triangle AYZ congruent? _ _ _ _ _ _

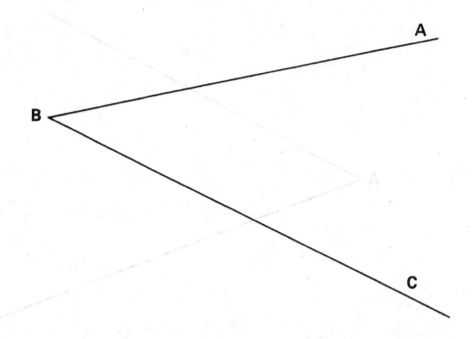

1. Draw a circle with B as center.

2. Label as D the intersection of $\overrightarrow{BA}$ and the circle.

3. Label as E the intersection of $\overrightarrow{BC}$ and the circle.

4. Draw segment $\overline{DE}$.

5. Construct an equilateral triangle with base DE.

6. Label as F the vertex of the triangle.

7. Draw $\overrightarrow{BF}$.

8. Check: Is angle ABF congruent to angle CBF? _ _ _ _ _

9. Does $\overrightarrow{BF}$ bisect angle ABC? _ _ _ _ _

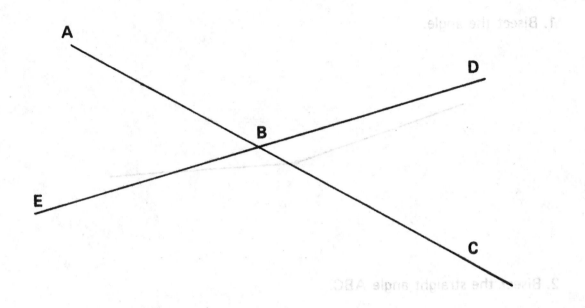

1. Compare angle ABE and angle DBC.

   Angle ABE is _ _ _ _ _ _ _ _ _ _ angle DBC.
   (a) larger than                     (c) congruent to
   (b) smaller than

2. Bisect angle ABE.

   Label as F any point on the <u>bisector</u>.

3. Extend $\overleftrightarrow{BF}$ to the right.

4. Does this line bisect angle DBC? _ _ _ _ _

# Right Angles

1. Bisect the angle.

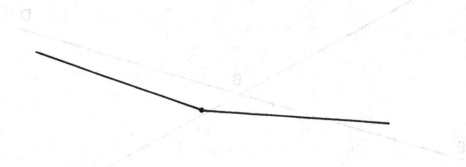

2. Bisect the straight angle ABC.

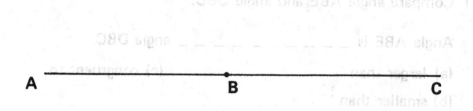

3. Label as D any point on the bisector.

4. Is angle ABD congruent to angle DBC? _ _ _ _ _

5. Angle ABD is a <u>right angle.</u>

   Angle DBC is also a right angle.

   A right angle is half a straight angle.

1. Check: Is angle WYX congruent to angle WYZ? _ _ _ _ _

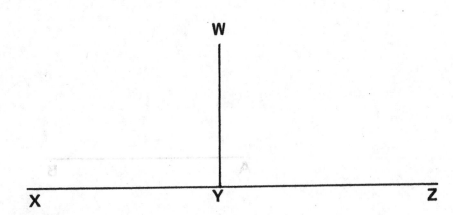

Are angles WYX and WYZ right angles? _ _ _ _ _

2. Extend line $\overleftrightarrow{BC}$ to the left.

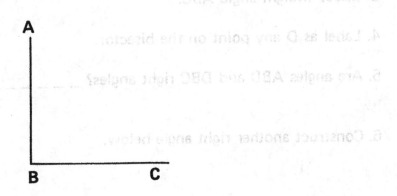

Check: Is angle ABC a right angle? _ _ _ _

Problem: *Construct a right angle.*

A ———————————————— B

Solution:

1. Extend line $\overleftrightarrow{AB}$ to the right.

2. Label as C any point on line $\overleftrightarrow{AB}$ to the right of B.

3. Bisect straight angle ABC.

4. Label as D any point on the bisector.

5. Are angles ABD and DBC right angles? _ _ _ _ _

6. Construct another right angle below.

# Perpendicular Lines

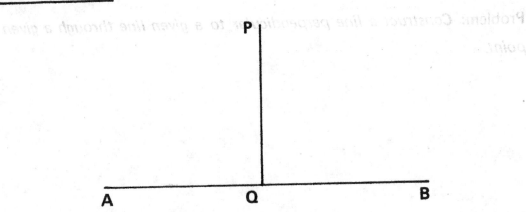

P

A              Q              B

1. Check:  Is angle PQA congruent to angle PQB? _ _ _ _ _

     Are angles PQA and PQB right angles? _ _ _ _ _

2. Two lines are <u>perpendicular</u> if they form right angles.

   Is $\overleftrightarrow{PQ}$ perpendicular to $\overrightarrow{AB}$? _ _ _ _ _

3. Check:  Is $\overleftrightarrow{MN}$ perpendicular to $\overrightarrow{ON}$? _ _ _ _ _

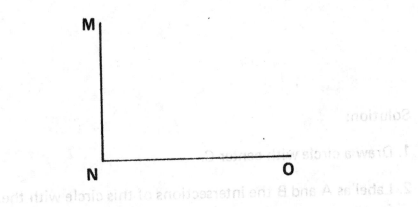

M

N                   O

4. Check:  Is $\overleftrightarrow{CD}$ perpendicular to $\overrightarrow{EF}$? _ _ _ _ _

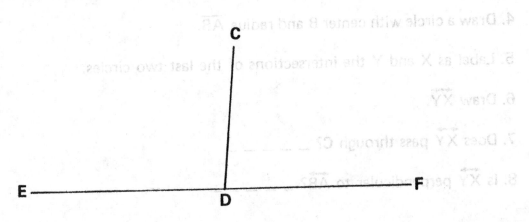

C

E _____ D _____ F

**Problem:** *Construct a line perpendicular to a given line through a given point.*

C

Solution:

1. Draw a circle with center C.

2. Label as A and B the intersections of this circle with the line.

3. Draw a circle with center A and radius $\overline{AB}$.

4. Draw a circle with center B and radius $\overline{AB}$.

5. Label as X and Y the intersections of the last two circles.

6. Draw $\overleftrightarrow{XY}$.

7. Does $\overleftrightarrow{XY}$ pass through C? _ _ _ _ _

8. Is $\overleftrightarrow{XY}$ perpendicular to $\overleftrightarrow{AB}$? _ _ _ _ _

**1. Construct a perpendicular to the given line through the given point.**

**2. Construct a perpendicular to the given line through the given point.**

28

A

1. Draw two small arcs with center A and congruent radii which intersect the line.

2. Label as P and Q these points of intersection.

3. Use a radius longer than segment $\overline{AP}$ to draw arcs with center P above and below line $\overleftrightarrow{PQ}$.

4. Use the same radius to draw arcs with center Q above and below line $\overleftrightarrow{PQ}$.

   Make the arcs with center Q intersect the arcs with center P.

5. Label the points of intersection R and S.

6. Draw $\overleftrightarrow{RS}$.

7. Does $\overleftrightarrow{RS}$ pass through point A? _ _ _ _ _

8. Check: Are angles RAQ and RAP right angles? _ _ _ _ _

9. Is line $\overleftrightarrow{RA}$ perpendicular to $\overleftrightarrow{PQ}$? _ _ _ _ _

# Review

1. Construct the perpendicular to each line through the given point.

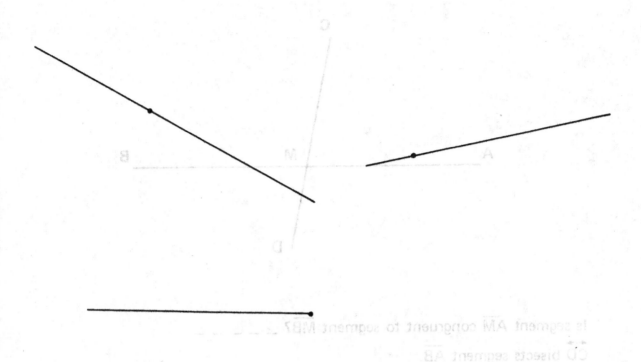

2. Bisect the angle.

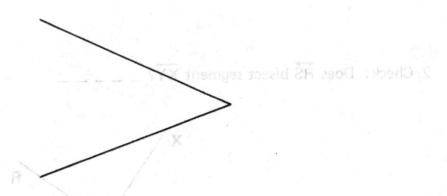

3. Compare the angles.

Are they congruent? _ _ _ _ _

# The Bisector of a Segment

1. Compare segments $\overline{AM}$ and $\overline{MB}$.

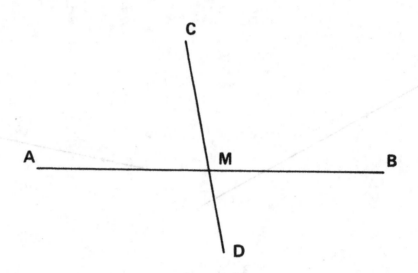

Is segment $\overline{AM}$ congruent to segment $\overline{MB}$? _ _ _ _ _

$\overleftrightarrow{CD}$ bisects segment $\overline{AB}$.

M is the midpoint of $\overline{AB}$.

2. Check: Does $\overleftrightarrow{RS}$ bisect segment $\overline{XY}$? _ _ _ _ _

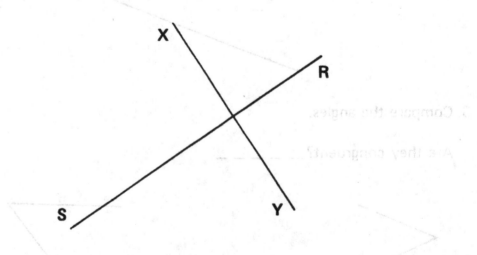

3. Does $\overleftrightarrow{XY}$ bisect segment $\overline{RS}$? _ _ _ _ _

Problem: *Bisect a given segment.*

A ————————————————————— B

Solution:

1. Draw a large arc with center A.

2. Use the same radius to draw a large arc with center B.
   Make these arcs intersect above and below $\overleftrightarrow{AB}$.

3. Label the points of intersection C and D.

4. Draw $\overleftrightarrow{CD}$.

5. Check: Does $\overleftrightarrow{CD}$ bisect segment $\overline{AB}$? _ _ _ _ _

6. Label as F the midpoint of segment $\overline{AB}$.

1. Bisect segment $\overline{AB}$.

A ————————————————————— B

2. Label the bisector as $\overleftrightarrow{CD}$.

3. Label the point of intersection M.

4. Fold your paper on $\overleftrightarrow{CD}$.

   Is segment $\overline{AM}$ congruent to segment $\overline{MB}$? _ _ _ _ _ _

   Is M the midpoint of $\overline{AB}$? _ _ _ _ _ _

5. Bisect the given segments.

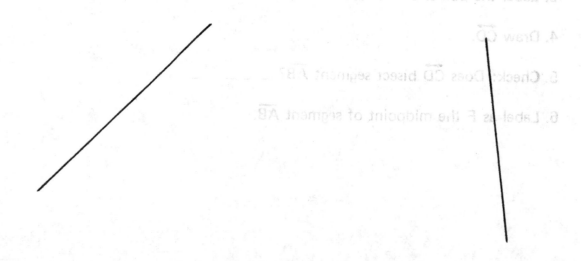

1. Draw a large arc with center A and radius $\overline{AB}$.

A ——————————————— B

2. Draw a large arc with center B and radius $\overline{AB}$.

   Make these arcs intersect in two points.

3. Label as C and D the points of intersection.

4. Draw $\overleftrightarrow{CD}$.

5. $\overleftrightarrow{CD}$ _ _ _ _ _ _ _ _ _ _ $\overline{AB}$.

   (a) draws                (c) is congruent to

   (b) bisects

6. Draw $\overline{AC}$, $\overline{AD}$, $\overline{BC}$, and $\overline{BD}$.

7. Are segments $\overline{AC}$, $\overline{AD}$, $\overline{BC}$, and $\overline{BD}$ all congruent? _ _ _ _ _

8. Is triangle ABC an equilateral triangle? _ _ _ _ _

9. Is triangle ABD an equilateral triangle? _ _ _ _ _

1. Double the given segment.

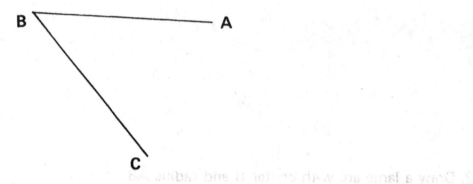

2. Connect A and C.

3. Bisect segment $\overline{AC}$. Label the midpoint as D.

4. Draw $\overrightarrow{BD}$.

5. Compare angle ABD and angle DBC.

6. Angle ABD is _ _ _ _ _ _ _ _ _ _ _ angle DBC.

    (a) larger than                  (c) congruent to

    (b) smaller than

1. Draw $\overline{PQ}$.

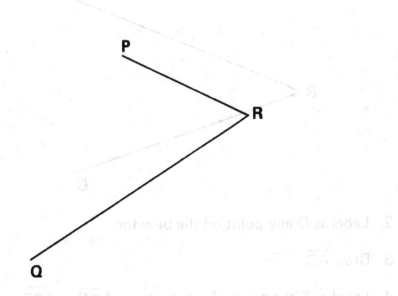

2. Bisect $\overline{PQ}$. Label the midpoint as M.

3. Draw $\overrightarrow{RM}$.

4. Fold your paper on $\overrightarrow{RM}$.

   Is angle MRP congruent to angle MRQ? _ _ _ _ _

5. Does $\overrightarrow{RM}$ bisect angle PRQ? _ _ _ _ _

6. Bisect the given angle.

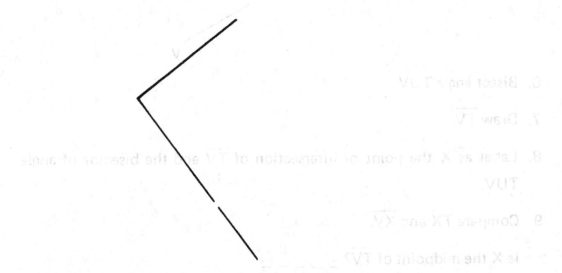

1. Bisect angle ABC.

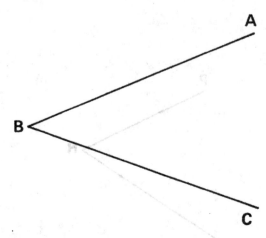

2. Label as D any point on the bisector.

3. Draw $\overline{AC}$.

4. Label as E the point of intersection of $\overline{AC}$ and $\overrightarrow{BD}$.

5. Is E the midpoint of $\overline{AC}$? _ _ _ _ _

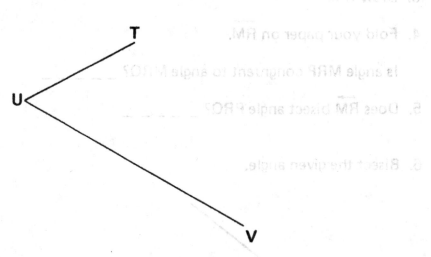

6. Bisect angle TUV.

7. Draw $\overline{TV}$.

8. Label as X the point of intersection of $\overline{TV}$ and the bisector of angle TUV.

9. Compare $\overline{TX}$ and $\overline{XV}$.

   Is X the midpoint of $\overline{TV}$? _ _ _ _ _ _

# The Perpendicular Bisector of a Segment

1. Bisect segment $\overline{AB}$.

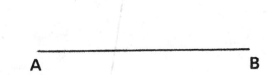

A _____ B

2. Label as C the midpoint of $\overline{AB}$.

3. Choose another point on the bisector line and label it D.

4. Fold your paper on $\overleftrightarrow{CD}$.

   Is segment $\overline{AC}$ congruent to segment $\overline{BC}$? _ _ _ _ _

   Does $\overleftrightarrow{CD}$ bisect segment $\overline{AB}$? _ _ _ _ _

5. Is angle ACD congruent to angle BCD? _ _ _ _ _

   Are angles ACD and BCD right angles? _ _ _ _ _

   Is $\overleftrightarrow{CD}$ perpendicular to $\overleftrightarrow{AB}$? _ _ _ _ _

6. $\overleftrightarrow{CD}$ is the <u>perpendicular bisector</u> of segment $\overline{AB}$.

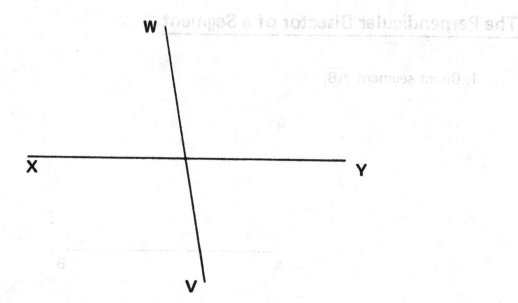

1. Does $\overleftrightarrow{WV}$ bisect segment $\overline{XY}$? _ _ _ _ _

Is $\overleftrightarrow{WV}$ perpendicular to $\overleftrightarrow{XY}$? _ _ _ _ _

Is $\overleftrightarrow{WV}$ the perpendicular bisector of segment $\overline{XY}$? _ _ _ _ _

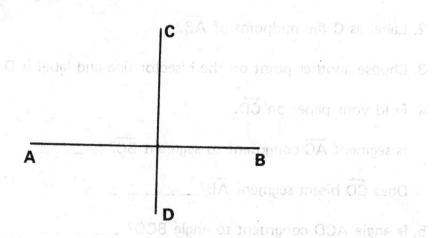

2. Is $\overleftrightarrow{CD}$ the perpendicular bisector of segment $\overline{AB}$? _ _ _ _ _

3. Is $\overleftrightarrow{MN}$ the perpendicular bisector of segment $\overline{PQ}$? _ _ _ _ _

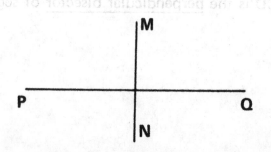

Problem: *Construct the perpendicular bisector of a given segment.*

K ——————————— L

**Solution:**

1. Draw a large arc with center K.

2. Use a congruent radius to draw a large arc with center L. Make the arcs intersect in two points.

3. Label the points of intersection as U and V.

4. Draw $\overleftrightarrow{UV}$.

5. Does $\overleftrightarrow{UV}$ bisect segment $\overline{KL}$? _ _ _ _ _

    Is $\overleftrightarrow{UV}$ perpendicular to $\overleftrightarrow{KL}$? _ _ _ _ _

    Is $\overleftrightarrow{UV}$ the perpendicular bisector of segment $\overline{KL}$? _ _ _ _ _

6. Construct the perpendicular bisector of segment $\overline{EF}$.

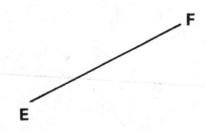

**1. Construct the perpendicular bisector of the given segment.**

**2. Construct perpendiculars to the given lines through the given points.**

**1. Draw the perpendicular bisectors of the three sides of the triangle.**

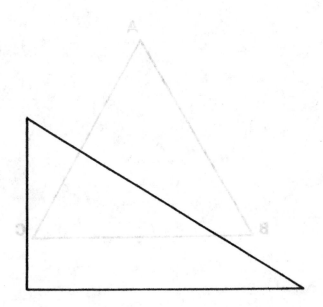

**2. Do the three perpendicular bisectors meet in a point? _ _ _ _ _**

1. Check:  Is the triangle ABC an equilateral triangle? _ _ _ _ _

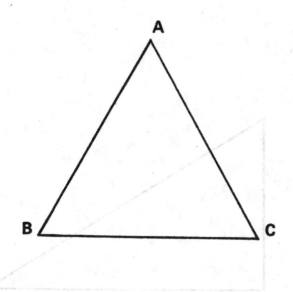

2. Bisect angle BAC.

Make the bisector intersect $\overline{BC}$.

3. Label the point of intersection D.

4. Check:  Does $\overrightarrow{AD}$ bisect side $\overline{BC}$? _ _ _ _ _

Check:  Is $\overleftrightarrow{AD}$ perpendicular to $\overleftrightarrow{BC}$? _ _ _ _ _

Is $\overrightarrow{AD}$ the perpendicular bisector of $\overline{BC}$? _ _ _ _ _

1. Construct an equilateral triangle with the given base.

X ——————————————————— Y

Label the other vertex Z.

2. Construct the perpendicular bisector of $\overline{XY}$.

   Label as M the midpoint of segment $\overline{XY}$.

3. Does the perpendicular bisector pass through vertex Z? _ _ _ _ _

4. Compare angle XZM and angle YZM.

   Does the perpendicular bisector bisect angle XZY? _ _ _ _ _

# Review

1. Compare the two angles. Which is larger? _ _ _ _ _ _

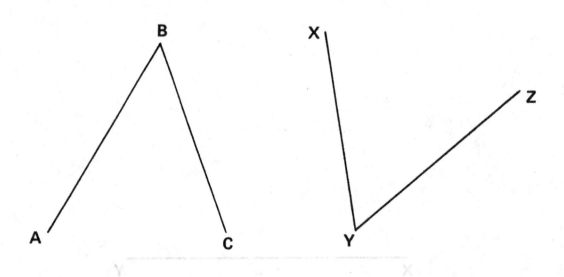

2. Bisect the given angles.

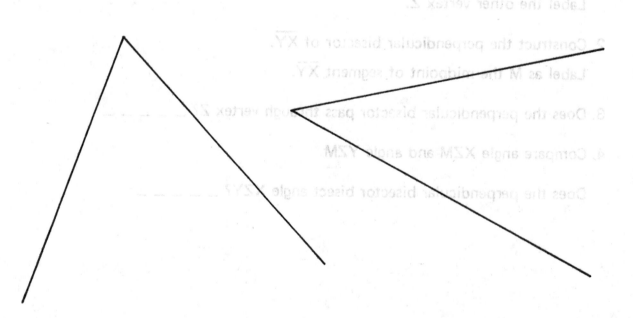

Draw perpendicular bisectors of the line segments.

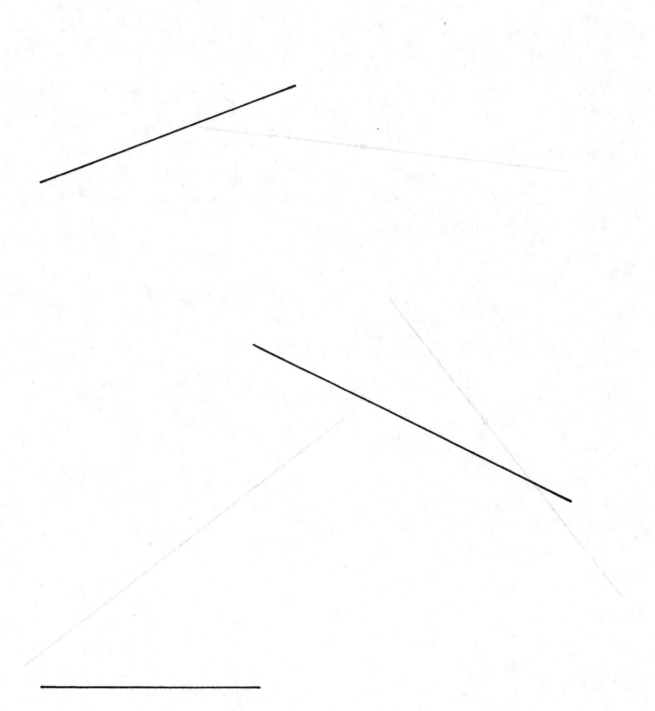

Construct the perpendicular to each line through the given point.

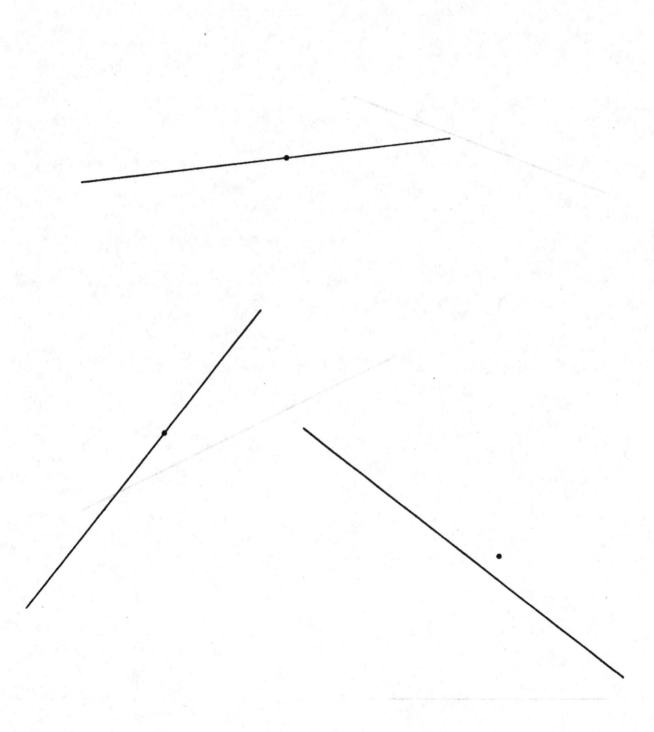

# Constructing the Perpendicular to a Line

**Problem:** *Construct a line perpendicular to a given line through a given point not on the line.*

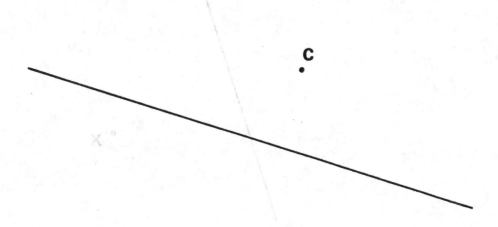

**Solution:**

1. Draw an arc with center C which intersects the line in two points.

2. Label as A and B the points of intersection.

3. Construct the perpendicular bisector of segment $\overline{AB}$.

4. Does the perpendicular bisector of segment $\overline{AB}$ pass through C? _ _ _ _ _

**1. Through point X construct a line perpendicular to the given line.**

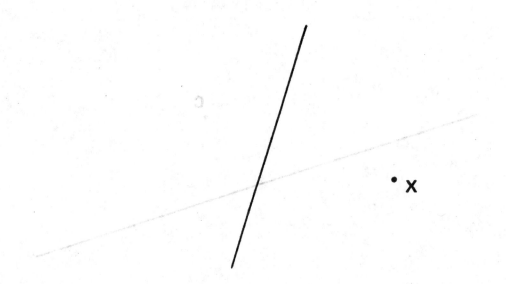

**2. Construct a line perpendicular to the given line through point Y on the given line.**

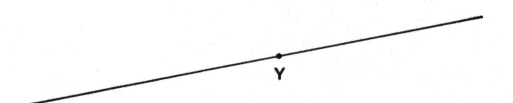

1. Construct through vertex A a line perpendicular to the <u>opposite</u> side of the triangle.


2. Now construct through vertices B and C lines perpendicular to their opposite sides.

   (Hint: Extend sides $\overline{AC}$ and $\overline{AB}$.)

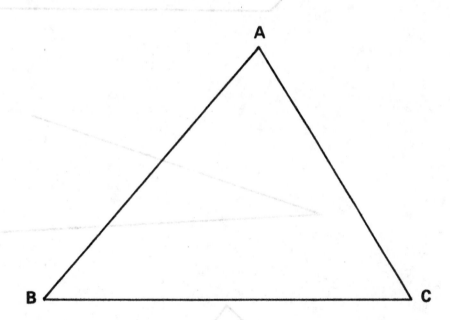

3. Do the three constructed lines all meet in a point? _ _ _ _ _

## Review

**Bisect the angles.**

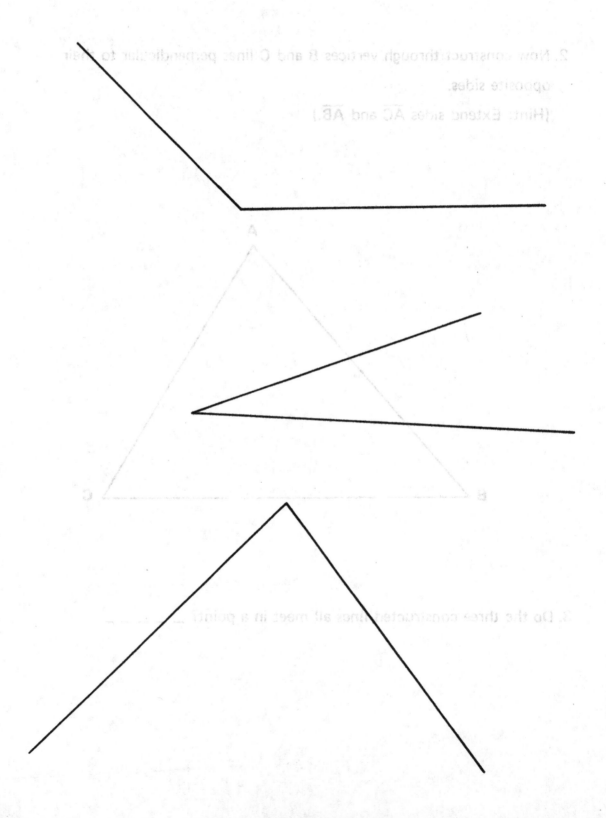

**1. Construct a line perpendicular to the given line through point X.**

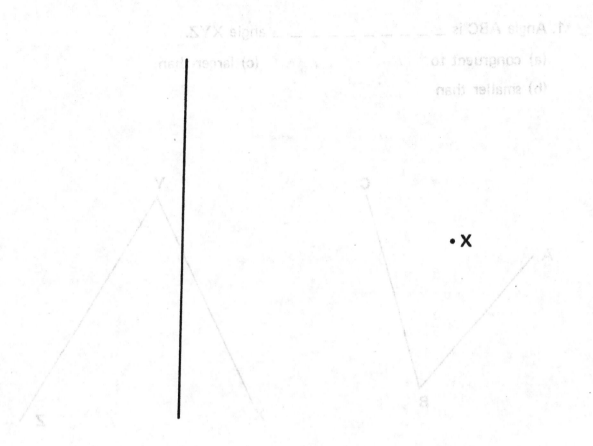

**2. Construct a line perpendicular to $\overleftrightarrow{XZ}$ through point Y.**

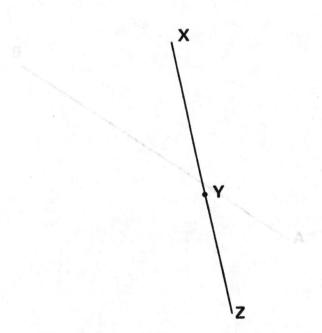

1. Angle ABC is _ _ _ _ _ _ _ _ _ _ angle XYZ.

    (a) congruent to                 (c) larger than

    (b) smaller than

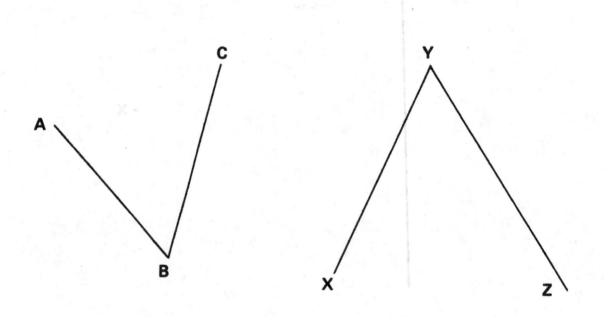

2. Divide segment $\overline{AB}$ into four congruent parts.

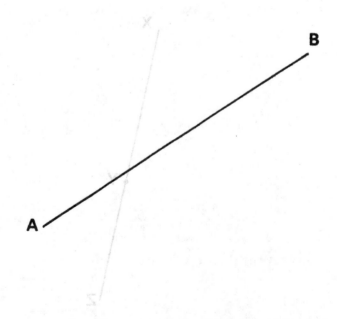

# Practice Test

1. Bisect angle XYZ.

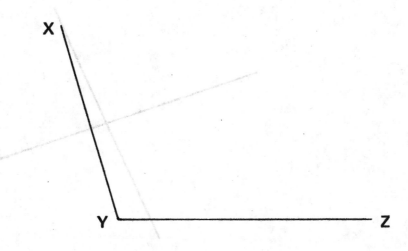

2. Construct through point P a line perpendicular to the given line.

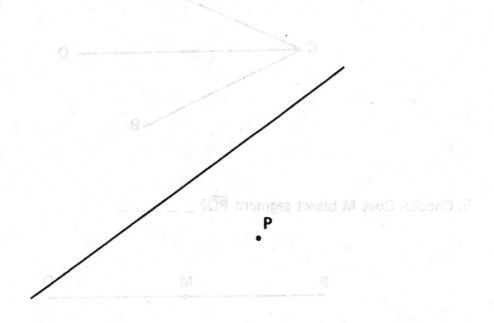

3. Check: Are the lines perpendicular? _ _ _ _ _

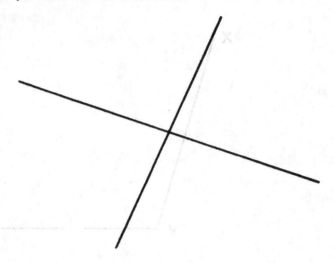

4. Check: Does $\overrightarrow{CD}$ bisect angle ACB? _ _ _ _ _

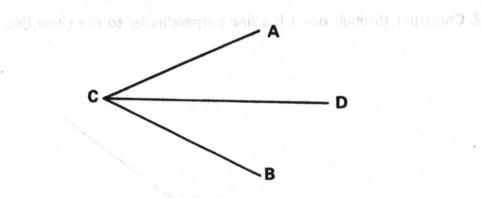

5. Check: Does M bisect segment $\overline{PQ}$? _ _ _ _ _ _

6. Triple the given line segment.

**7.** Construct a line perpendicular to segment $\overline{MN}$ through point P.

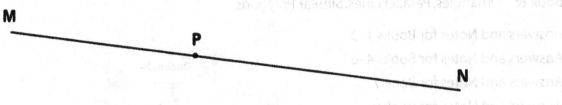

**8.** Construct the perpendicular bisector of the given segment.

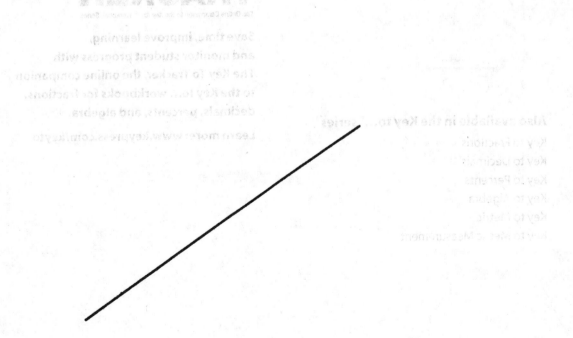

# Key to Geometry® workbooks

Book 1:   Lines and Segments
Book 2:   Circles
Book 3:   Constructions
Book 4:   Perpendiculars
Book 5:   Squares and Rectangles
Book 6:   Angles
Book 7:   Perpendiculars and Parallels, Chords and Tangents, Circles
Book 8:   Triangles, Parallel Lines, Similar Polygons

Answers and Notes for Books 1–3
Answers and Notes for Books 4–6
Answers and Notes for Book 7
Answers and Notes for Book 8

## The Key To TRACKER™

The Online Companion to the *Key to...*® Workbook Series

**Save time, improve learning, and monitor student progress with The Key To Tracker, the online companion to the Key to... workbooks for fractions, decimals, percents, and algebra.**

**Learn more: www.keypress.com/keyto**

## Also available in the Key to...® series

Key to Fractions®
Key to Decimals®
Key to Percents®
Key to Algebra®
Key to Metric®
Key to Metric Measurement®

## Key Curriculum Press
### INNOVATORS IN MATHEMATICS EDUCATION

ISBN 978-0-913684-74-0